The Philosophy of Native American Circles

By
Susan Thomas Underwood

Published by:
O-SI-YO Truthart Publisher
Rural Route 1, Box 188A
Delaware, Oklahoma 74027
Truthart.net

Dedication

I wish to dedicate this book to my husband, Donald Joseph Underwood. He not only supports my painting and writing, but follows through with me in traveling the country to show it and sell it.. Thank you, my dear husband for your support in all that I do.

Publishing Information

The Philosophy of Native American Circles
Text and Illustrations Copyright 2005 by
Susan Thomas Underwood. All rights reserved.

This First Edition: limited edition of 500 copies, signed and numbered on acid-free paper with archival inks.

ISBN # 0-976-7254-0-1

The Philosophy of Native American Circles
Susan Thomas Underwood
Printed in the United States of America

Contents

Introductions 1

The Shapes. 2

The Motions. 6

The Cycles. 10

Relationships 16

Actions & Reactions 22

We Are All Related. 28

Manifestations. 34

Opposites. 40

Conclusion. 49

The Circle is sacred to America's
Indigenous People.

To them, the Circle embodies the center of wisdom,

The center of the Universe.

It is the heart of our Creator,
and the place from where all things
begin.

The Shapes

They perpetuate life...

Look up to the sky beings

and see their shapes...

The moon, the stars, the planets, and the life giving sun. All are perfect spheres... Perfect circles.

Look now to thine own body and see the circles of life:
The womb,

       The egg,

              The ovary, and

                      The testicle.

See the circle of the single cell. Life begins within these magical circles.

The Motions

The spiral marks the beginning for all things

in the universe...

Space particles move in a spiral to create new stars and galaxies. The Sky Beings rotate in circles and orbit in circles.

The spiral marks the beginning for all Earth Beings. The spiral of DNA marks the beginning of life and intelligence for all life forms including plants, insects, and mammals.

The spiral, too marks the movement of the elements: That of wind becomes the whirlwind, tornado, and the hurricane. That of sound vibrates out in perfect circular waves, as do ripples of water. Moreover, movement of water creates the spiraling whirlpool.

The Cycles

They revolve in circles....

For example, the cycle of water begins, say. . With the pool. The pool's water evaporates to the sky as a vaporous cloud, which condenses back into rain, which falls back to the Earth, returning water into the pool.

Minerals cycle within the earth and upwards to the surface through lava flowing from a volcano. It cools into rock which gradually erodes into soil, becoming pressurized as more soil covers it and eventually it becomes sedimentary rock. As the sedimentary rock becomes further buried within the earth, it is pressurized and heated, turning into marble, granite, and finally back into lava which may return again to the earth's surface through the volcano.

"The cycle of life (substance) begins as minerals feed the plants, who in turn feed the grass eaters (herbivores), who in turn feed the meat eaters (carnivores), who in turn die and decay back into earth, thus becoming mineral again.. This return to the earth is true for all things that rise up from the earth, whether it be mineral (a rock breaks down into soil), plant or animal,. All things break down and become earth again. Even a machine or building that is created by man will eventually give way to the rusting process and return once again to the our mother, the Earth.

The cycle of soul begins as spirit in the spirit world. At some point spirit is born into a physical body and travels through youth, adulthood and productivity (which can be offspring or a body of work), then aging and finally death. Upon death, the soul once again returns to the spirit world.

Relationships

Relationships of human beings (or the "two leggeds")
form circles of inter-dependence upon each other...

Male and female love forms a circle of unity. The female gives from her heart, manifested physically as breast milk, as the male receives through his. The male gives from his loins, manifested physically as semen, as the female receives through hers. Their circle of unity is perpetuated through the act of making love.

Any relationship whether two legged or four, winged or finned, is created from a balance of facilitation, or co-dependency. The act of giving, or helping, cannot exist outside that of receiving something back; nor can the act of receiving exist outside that of giving something back.

For example, a bowl full of candy can give out candy so long as there is candy to give. Once it becomes empty, the bowl must receive candy before it can give out again. Relationships are subject to the same law of giving and receiving. When they become out of balance, the circle is broken and the cycle is not able to continue. Whether one party voluntarily decides to stop giving until something is given back, or whether the party becomes depleted and can no longer continue to give, the cycle will ultimately be broken.

Parent and child love forms a circle of facilitation. As the parent births a child and nurtures it through childhood, the parent has facilitated the new soul from the spirit world and into the physical world. As the parent becomes aged and needy, the child nurtures the parent and facilitates the translation from the physical world and back into the spirit world through the dieing process. A circle has been completed.

The mother, in blue, assists the new soul into this world through physical birthing and nurturing. The child, in purple, assists the mature soul back into the spirit world through nurturing through the death process.

Actions &

Reactions

Actions create reactions that perpetuate a fluid circle of energy...

Energy never goes away, it simply changes form. For example, a speeding car may seem to be consuming energy without giving it back out. However, as it cuts through and displaces the air, wind is created. The wind goes into the atmosphere and eventually becomes part of a storm. The storm at some point may pass through a wind generator, creating electricity. The electricity may be used to refine oil into gasoline that will in turn re-fuel the car. Hence, the scientific law, "every action causes an equal reaction".

Such fluid circles of action and reaction are present within our own behavior, such as the spiritual law of Karma. Karma can be simplified into the well known phrase, "What goes around, comes around". No matter what religion one subscribes to, most observe this principle of the circle. When we put out good things, good things will come back to us. When we put out bad

Things, they too, come back to us. Hence the phrase, "Those who live by the sword, die by the sword".

Of course, occasionally bad things happen to good people, and good things happen to bad people. Collectively speaking, however, we can all see the circle revolve as our actions ultimately come back around to us.

Acts of remorse and forgiveness are intertwined. When a person gives out remorse, it becomes easy to forgive him. Without the act of remorse it becomes very difficult to forgive. We almost lack the ability to forgive without first receiving remorse, and it may be considered a gift of Divine grace when we are *given* the gallant ability to forgive in the absence of remorse.

WE are all Related

The existence of all circle shapes, motions, cycles, relationships and behaviors create a huge circle of co-dependence for all things in the universe.

Each component of the Universal Circle has its own purpose. For example, even the sky beings support our circle of life here on earth. The sun not only nourishes and warms all things, but also serves as timekeeper in the keeping of the hours that turn into days.

The moon not only lights our night sky, but also creates gravitational pull which creates our tides and cycles which give us the monthly cycles for our calendar.

Minerals; the rocks and the soil, cycle within our Mother Earth and record events from past ages. Skeletons and artifacts of living things fall to the soil and eventually become buried with new soil. Indeed, modern day science looks to sedimentary layers of soil and rock to tell the true story of our earth and living beings of the past. This is why the

Native Americans attribute the Rock People as "keepers of wisdom" who record the history of our Mother Earth.

The Plant Tribe not only feeds, clothes and shelters the earth creatures, but creates our atmosphere with their breath, protects the soil with their roots, and holds the key to our medicinal healing.

The circle of inter-dependence spawns the Native American term, "we are all related". Not only do all things from sky to earth come from the same basic elements, but the actions of all things affect one another. If there is disruption with the sun or moon, soil or plants, two or four legged, winged or finned; chaos and sometimes disaster results.

Manifestations

The Native American people who realized circle wisdom honored the circle throughout their culture. .

Their symbol of worship, the medicine wheel, honors the four directions: North, East, South, and West; creating the circle of the wheel. Representative of each direction is a plant, animal, color, and component of wisdom. It is a wheel of balance of all things important to the Native Americans' symbolizing a balance between the physical world and that of spirit.

The circle is honored in Native American social and ceremonial dances. Dances take place within a circle and are preformed with circular motions and in circular directions. Some tribes dance in a clockwise direction, others circle counter-clockwise so as to follow the way of the natural spiral (for example, the whirlpool motion is counter-clockwise). The dance circle has a direction of entrance and exit (may differ with various tribal customs between East or West), in order that a complete spiral is made before exiting the circle. The act of leaving the circle without completing it is an act of dishonor to the circle.

Circle balance can be applied to almost everything that Natives do. Native American worship is balanced by the act of meditation, or "receiving the Word", as well as the act of prayer. This creates a complete circle of communication; that of giving (prayer) and that of receiving (meditation).

Wisdom from our elders gained through trial and error is passed back to the young in order to be preserved for coming generations. Such wisdom must be "Kept", thus the Native American term, "Wisdom Keeper", so that it is not necessary for each new generation to relearn hard earned wisdom. New wisdom is then learned by subsequent generations, creating a snowball effect as generational wisdom continually adds new wisdom to the old.

Opposites

In every component of our world, the acts of ourselves and of nature, there is a perfect balance within the wisdom of the circle. . .

Such balance is a rule in our universe and when we do not yield to it, we become out of balance. When we receive, we must balance that by giving. When we pray, we must balance that by meditation. When we work, we balance that with rest; and when we eat, we balance that by fasting (or not eating). We balance our learning by teaching to others and our talking by the act of listening to others.

Extreme ends of the circle create opposites that balance one another. For example, as the day cycles there are times of light and times of no light (darkness). It is evident that the circle creates infinite opposites between the existence of a thing and the non-existence of a thing. The existence of heat creates hot, and the non-existence of heat creates cold. The existence of good is countered with a non-existence of good, that of evil. Therefore, existence of a thing and its lack there of creates its complete opposite.

Contrasts, such as fire and ice, manifest harmony in our world of split positive and negatives. After all, everything comes from the ONE.

Might we extend this universal law to the existence of a living thing, such as an animal or plant species? When an animal or plant species is exterminated, what opposite is created? We may not even know, but we can assume the lack will surely reverberate through the universe and create an opposite reaction that will affect all. Now, how about our own lives?

Anyone who has experienced the death of a loved one knows the absence of that loved one, whether man or beast, creates a whole new reality for those left behind. The death is like hitting a great wall; the person that one is at the time the death is experienced simply cannot move forward any longer. In order to move forward, one is transformed through the cooping mechanisms they are forced to utilize in order to survive the death. Down the road a year or two, one realizes he/she is not the same person they were when their loved one died. The truth is that they have experienced the opposites within the law of the circle; the reality of the universe has changed.

One must strongly consider the opposites within circle wisdom when considering taking one's own life. While it may seem a valid solution in the moment, the ripple effect throughout the universe is infinite and one cannot even imagine the implications of such an act.

knowledge is power, and the knowledge of the law of the circle leaves a humanity that is respectful of one another. Indeed, a humanity that is respectful of the others with whom we share this circle we call Earth, whether it be the animal family, the plant family, or the mineral family. A humanity who respects the resources of the earth as they transform into energy and move from wind to water, from the earth's surface to within, and then up into the sky.

Such humanity would likely show this respect for the circle laws by mimicking the circle in all that they create, and in all that they do. They would probably build and reside with circular homes, dance within and in circles, worship within circles and create circular symbols for their beliefs, and honor the circle in every aspect of their behavior.

Such is the mind-set of a New Native American culture within our "melting Pot" America. Many, whether or not they have Native American blood, have found that the Native American philosophies add a dimension of balance to their already existing belief system.

Know Ye then, the wisdom of the circle

For it is the key to the wisdom of thy Universe,

And to The One who created it.

Works By
Susan Thomas Underwood

This book and other products listed below
are available through her studio at:

Underwood Studio
Rural Route 1, Box 188a
Delaware, Oklahoma 74027
1-877-249-2301
Website: truthart.net

Walk With Spirit: published 1998 1st ed. signed & numbered. 2nd open ed. 2001. $8.99 plus $2 shipping.

Seeks the Truth: Published 2000, 1st limited edition Signed & numbered. $10.99 plus $2 shipping.

Animals and Their Wisdom: published 2001, 1st limited edition 500 signed & numbered, 2004 open edition. $13.95 + $3 shipping.

Cherokee Heritage Calendar: current and back issues. Published yearly. Current issue $12.95 plus $4 shipping. Back issues $5 plus $3 shipping.

Cherokee Images Address & Cookbook: Published 2003 with images from Cherokee artists on letter pages with favorite recipes. $11.99 + 5 shipping.

About The Author

   Susan Thomas Underwood grew up on her family ranch in N.E. Oklahoma within the Cherokee Nation. Susan's Indian ancestors removed from the Eastern Cherokee into Texas and she is not eligible for membership with the Oklahoma Cherokee. She is a member of the N.E. Alabama Cherokee where her Cherokee ancestors originated.

   She grew up close to nature and her best friends were animals, both domestic and wild. She courted her high school sweetheart, Joe Thomas, who worked on the ranch and later married him in college. While married to Joe, they had two children and he later assumed operation of the ranch and Susan taught art in public schools for 17 years. Their marriage ended in 1991 when Mr. Thomas died of kidney cancer at age 42.

   Susan's life was drastically changed through this tragedy and she began painting Native American themes and attending art shows. In 1993, she married Donald Underwood and eventually dedicated all her time and efforts to writing and painting her spiritual messages. This book includes a retrospective of many years of work.